SICK AT SEA?

Cure it or cut it off!

Anna Claybourne

Crabtree Publishing Company

www.crabtreebooks.com

Author: Anna Claybourne
Editor: Kathy Middleton
Production coordinator: Ken Wright
Prepress technician: Margaret Amy Salter
Series consultant: Gill Matthews

Picture Credits:

Alamy Images: Medical-on-Line 25
Corbis: Historical Picture Archive 21
Getty Images: The Bridgeman Art Library 23t
Istockphoto: Grafissimo 28, Duncan Walker 13c
Library of Congress: 15
Photolibrary: 8b
Shutterstock: (Cover) Rimantas Abromas 27tr, Potapov Alexander 19t, Khomulo Anna 12t, Subbotina Anna 4b, ANP 24t, Davi Sales Batista 10t, Betacam-SP 6t, Cartoonhead 29t, Andraž Cerar 6b, Charlotte Erpenbeck 19b, Lagui 5c, Ledo 24b, LilKar 14b, Lilun 29b, Polina Lobanova 18l, Milos Luzanin 22t, Reha Mark 10b, Originalpunkt 14t, Orionmystery 7b, Michael Pemberton 18r, Pennyimages 12bl, Psamtik 17b,Koum Quat 4t, Tom Robbrecht 27b, Elena Schweitzer 8t, 27tl, Shoeberl 22b, Roman Sigaev 23b, Stocksnapp 26, SVLumagraphica 9, Michael Taylor 20t, Tohan 16, 27c, Vinata 12br, Yasna 5t, Marlena Zagajewska 13t
Wikimedia Commons: 5b, 11, Gaius Cornelius 20b, Magnus Manske 17t, Forest & Kim Starr 7t

Library and Archives Canada Cataloguing in Publication

Claybourne, Anna
Sick at sea? cure it or cut it off! / Anna Claybourne.

(Crabtree connections)
Includes index.
ISBN 978-0-7787-9901-6 (bound).--ISBN 978-0-7787-9922-1 (pbk.)

1. Medicine, Naval--History--18th century--Juvenile literature.
2. Materia medica, Vegetable--History--Juvenile literature. I. Title. II. Series: Crabtree connections

RC986.C53 2010 j616.9'8024 C2010-905074-6

Library of Congress Cataloging-in-Publication Data

Claybourne, Anna.
Sick at sea? cure it or cut it off! / Anna Claybourne.
p. cm. -- (Crabtree connections)
Includes index.
ISBN 978-0-7787-9922-1 (pbk. : alk. paper) -- ISBN 978-0-7787-9901-6 (reinforced library binding : alk. paper)
1. Environmentally induced diseases--Juvenile literature. I. Title.
RB152.5.C53 2011
616.9'8--dc22

2010030824

Crabtree Publishing Company

www.crabtreebooks.com 1-800-387-7650

Printed in the U.S.A./082010/WO20101210

Published in Canada
Crabtree Publishing
616 Welland Ave.
St. Catharines, Ontario
L2M 5V6

Published in the United States
Crabtree Publishing
PMB 59051
350 Fifth Avenue, 59th Floor
New York, New York 10118

Contents

Welcome Aboard!

Welcome to a life of danger, disaster, and deadly disease! As a ship's **surgeon** in the 1700s, you won't just hand out cough syrup and bandages. No! You'll fix broken bones, pull out teeth, and **lance** boils. You will also chop off rotting legs, dig out bullets, and sew up wounds. Let's hope you have nerves of steel!

Your medicine chest

Every ship's surgeon needs a well-stocked medicine chest. Here are some of the things it should contain:

Medicines

- aloe vera
- chamomile
- cinnamon
- clove oil
- dragon's blood
- honey
- lavender
- licorice
- mercury pills
- mint
- mustard
- myrrh
- **opium**
- peppermint
- Peruvian bark
- rhubarb
- rosemary
- squill
- turpentine
- vinegar
- wormwood

mint

Tools and supplies

- bandages
- blood bowls
- **cauterizing** irons
- cloths
- **forceps**
- head saw
- knives and razors
- needles and thread
- **pestle and mortar**
- pliers
- **probes**
- scissors
- weighing scales

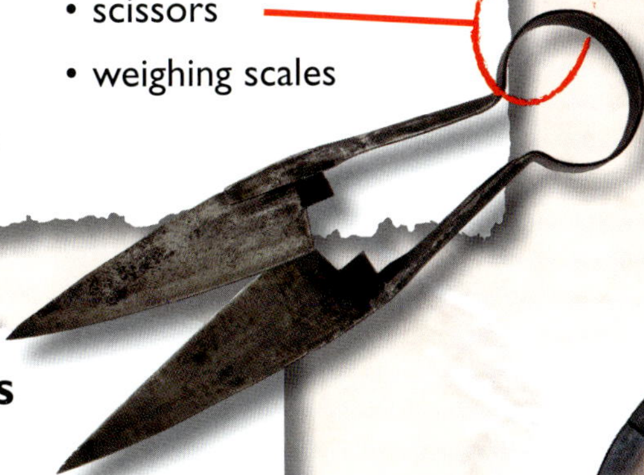

The surgeon's sick bay

Your ship has a special **sick bay**, where you can keep an eye on sailors who aren't feeling well. Each day you should

- check on your patients;
- prepare and hand out medicines;
- do urgent operations;
- keep the sick bay clean.

The famous pirate Blackbeard once demanded a medicine chest in return for setting some hostages free!

Blackbeard knew his pirate crew were worth their weight in gold. Keeping them healthy was important.

Cabin Fever

As your ship sails around the world, the sailors will pick up all kinds of nasty germs and bugs. These come from dirty water, bad food, and local people. Many of these germs cause a **fever**, or high temperature. Once the fever has passed, your patient may get better. But, watch out for **malaria**—it can be a killer!

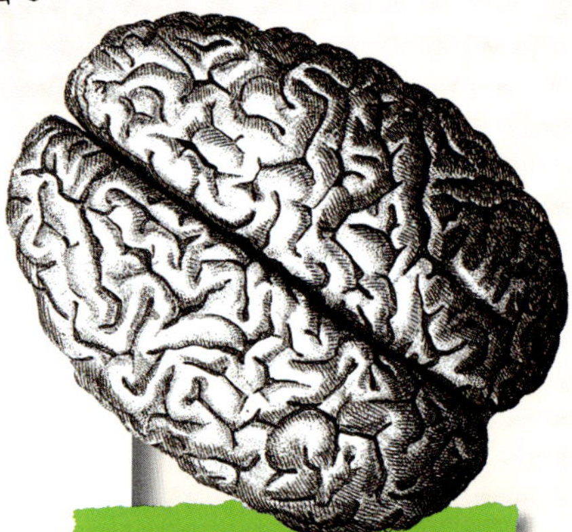

Fever affects the brain and can cause **hallucinations**.

Fever treatments

Treat fever with one of these remedies.

Wormwood

This herb has been used since ancient times. Give the patient salts of wormwood, made from ashes collected after burning the plant.

Mercury

Pills containing **mercury** are a cure for fever.

Vinegar

If you run out of other medicines, try a spoonful of vinegar.

Modern scientists know that mercury is actually a poison! But, hundreds of years ago, it was used as a medicine.

mercury

Malaria treatment

The best cure for malaria is Peruvian bark, from the cinchona tree. Here's how to use it:

1. Use dried, powdered Peruvian bark.
2. The patient will suffer high fevers with **chills** in between.
3. Give one **dram** of bark **tonic** every hour during the chills.

The cinchona tree grows in South America.

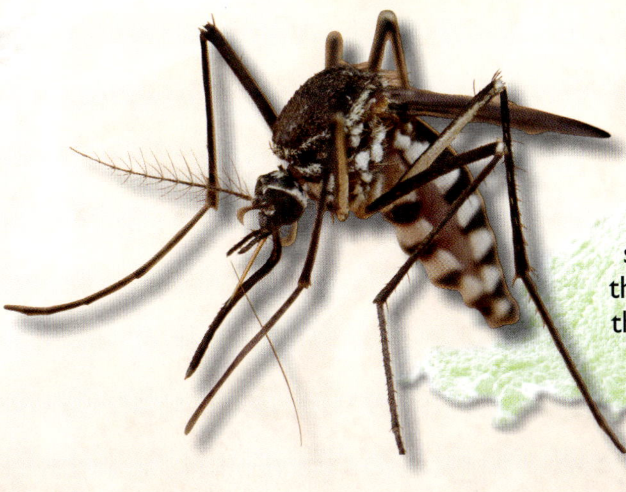

Top Tips

Watch out for striped mosquitoes like this one. They're the ones that spread malaria when they suck your blood.

Terrible Toothache

There's no such thing as toothpaste, so you'll spend plenty of time looking at stinky, rotten teeth. Quite often, you'll have to pull them out, too. Get your pliers ready!

Cloves are the dried flower buds of a type of tree.

Treatment for toothache

You will need:

- clove oil
- cloth

How to do it

1. Soak the cloth in clove oil.
2. Fold it up tightly.
3. Press the cloth against the bad tooth, and shut the patient's mouth to hold it in place.

You'll need a firm grip to pull teeth out!

Taking a tooth out

You will need:

- grippers or pliers
- cloth
- vinegar

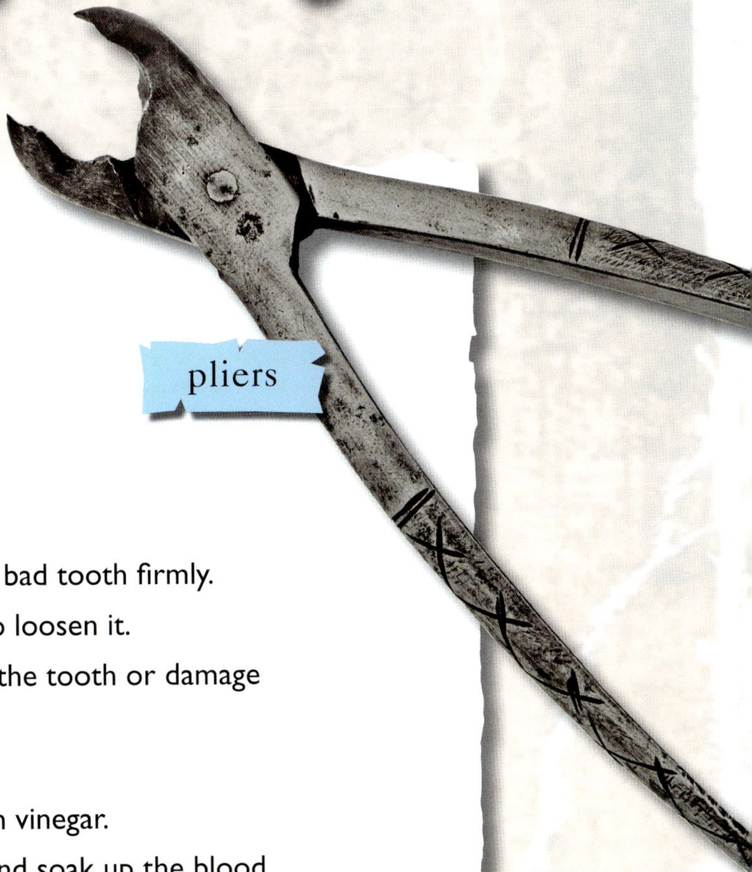

How to do it

1. Use the pliers to grip the bad tooth firmly.
2. Twist the tooth around to loosen it.
3. Be careful not to shatter the tooth or damage nearby healthy teeth!
4. Pull the tooth out.
5. Wash the mouth out with vinegar.
6. Use cloth to fill the gap and soak up the blood.

Bad teeth

Many 18th-century sailors have rotten teeth and bad breath. Many diseases, such as scurvy (see page 26), not only make you sick, they can make teeth go bad.

Falls and Fractures

Arrrrrggggghh! THUD!!!
What was that?
It was probably one of the sailors falling off the **rigging** and hitting the deck. If he survived, it is likely he'll have horrible injuries. You must be ready to fix them.

Setting a broken bone

You will need:

- a splint, such as a piece of wood
- bandages
- pain-killing medicine

How to do it

1. Give the patient a painkiller, such as opium or rum.
2. Gently pull the broken arm or leg to straighten it. Ouch!
3. Lay the splint along the broken limb.
4. Bandage the splint to the limb tightly.

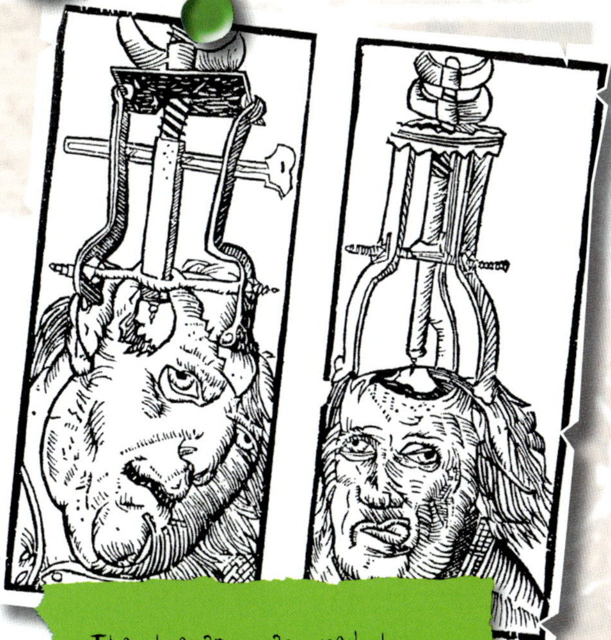

The trepan was used to drill holes in a person's skull.

Fixing a smashed skull

You will need:

- cloths and seawater
- a knife or chisel
- a head saw or **trepan**
- bandages

How to do it

1. Wash the head with seawater.
2. Pull out any smashed-in sections of skull and pick out bone splinters.
3. Use the head saw to cut off any pieces of bone sticking out.
4. If there is swelling, you must use the trepan. It will make a hole in the skull to release blood inside.
5. Bandage up the head.

Man overboard!

Surprisingly, many sailors aren't good swimmers. If they go overboard, they begin to sink! To treat a drowned man, hold him upside down and shake him well to remove water from his lungs.

Stomach Bugs

On board ship you'll see lots of vomiting and diarrhea. **Seasickness**, rotten food, and germs can give sailors stomach bugs. Luckily, you have lots of handy sickness medicines in your medicine chest.

A cure for vomiting

You can use flavored water called "aquae" to treat sickness. You will need:

- ginger root, aniseed, cinnamon, or peppermint
- boiling water
- clean cloth

How to do it

1. Stir the herb or root you are using into the hot water.
2. Leave the mixture to cool.
3. Strain the water through a cloth to remove the pieces.
4. Give the patient a glass of the medicine every hour.

Peppermint and ginger (below) are both good for sickness.

rhubarb

Treating diarrhea

Diseases, such as **cholera**, can cause diarrhea as well as vomiting. To treat diarrhea, you will need:

- dried rhubarb
- wine
- cloths

How to do it

1. Stir the rhubarb into the wine.
2. Give the patient a glass of the medicine, then send him to rest in bed.
3. Warm the cloths by the fire and lay them over the patient's stomach.

Lord Nelson

Seasick admiral

English admiral Lord Horatio Nelson spent his life at sea. Although he loved ships, he suffered from terrible seasickness. He often had to stay in his bed for days on end.

Coughs and Colds

You might think coughs and colds aren't that serious. But a nasty cold or flu bug is bad news at sea. It can put most of the crew out of action.

medicine bottle

Syrup of squills cure

This cold **remedy** is made from a seashore plant called squill. It's good for chest colds, stuffed-up noses, and sore throats.

You will need:

- squill **extract**
- honey
- sugar

How to do it

1. Stir the ingredients together to make a thick syrup.
2. Give the patient a large spoonful three times a day.

Honey has been used for centuries to soothe sore throats and kill germs.

Explorers spread dangerous cold and flu germs to the Taino people of the Caribbean in the 1490s.

Healing a headache

- Soak chamomile flowers in water to make a soothing drink.
- Place a warmed cup upside down on the head. As it cools, it will suck the skin. This is called "cupping." It is thought to cure all kinds of aches and pains.
- Try syrup of **ipecac**, which comes from a plant root. It will make your patient vomit, but his headache might go away!

Spreading germs

Explorers from Europe first sailed to the New World in the late 1400s. They took cold and flu germs with them and passed them to the native people. Many of them died. They had never had these germs before and their bodies were not used to fighting them.

Lancing a Boil

Boils happen when germs and dirt collect under the skin and swell up. Boils are common at sea, where sailors live crowded together in dirty conditions. Some boils get bigger and bigger until they POP! Others have to be lanced, or sliced open.

A ship makes a great home for boil germs!

Plaster for a boil

A **plaster** is an **ointment**-like mixture. You put one on a boil to make **pus** come to the surface and burst out. You will need:

- lard
- oil
- mustard
- a piece of cloth

How to do it

1. Mix the ingredients together over a fire.
2. Smear the warm mixture onto the cloth.
3. Lay the cloth plaster-side down over the boil.

Lancing a boil

So the boil hasn't popped? It's time to lance it. You will need:

- seawater
- a small, sharp knife
- turpentine
- cloths
- bandage

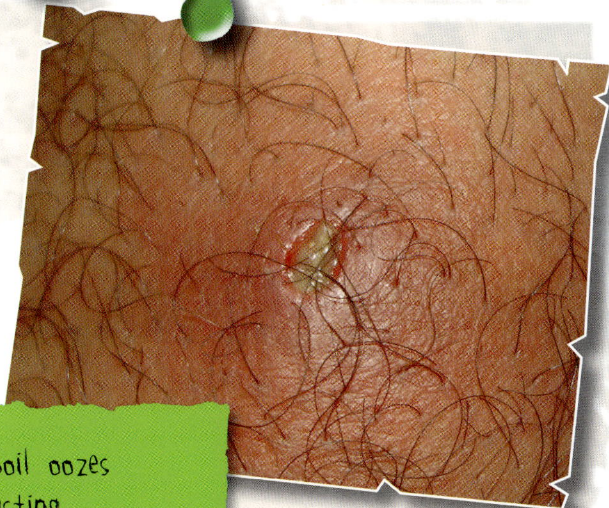

A boil oozes disgusting yellow pus.

How to do it

1. Wash the area with seawater.
2. Slice the boil open with a knife and squeeze it.
3. Use the cloths to soak up the pus and blood. Yuck!
4. Wash the area with turpentine.
5. Bandage the wound until it heals over.

Turpentine is made of juice or sap from a pine tree.

Turpentine is a good germ-killer, but warn your patient that it may sting and burn!

Battle Wounds

A good ship's surgeon must always be ready for a pirate attack! With their razor-sharp swords and deadly guns, pirates can cause some nasty wounds. Even if your crew fights them off, you'll have lots of injuries to deal with.

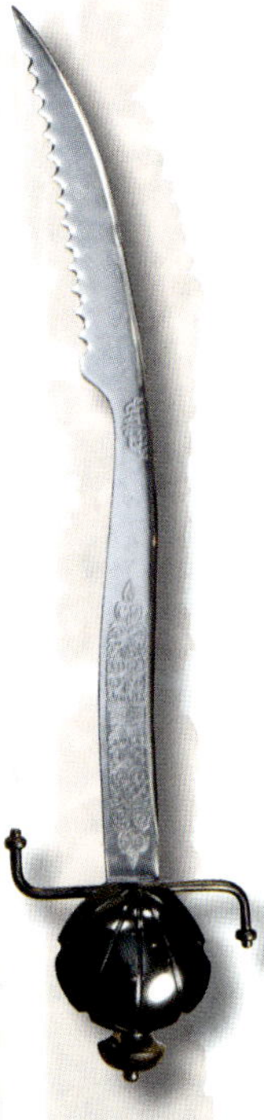

Treatment for a sword or dagger wound

You will need:

- dragon's blood powder
- wine or oil
- pestle and mortar
- a piece of wood
- needle
- waxed thread

A pestle and mortar is perfect for crushing ingredients to make medicines and ointments.

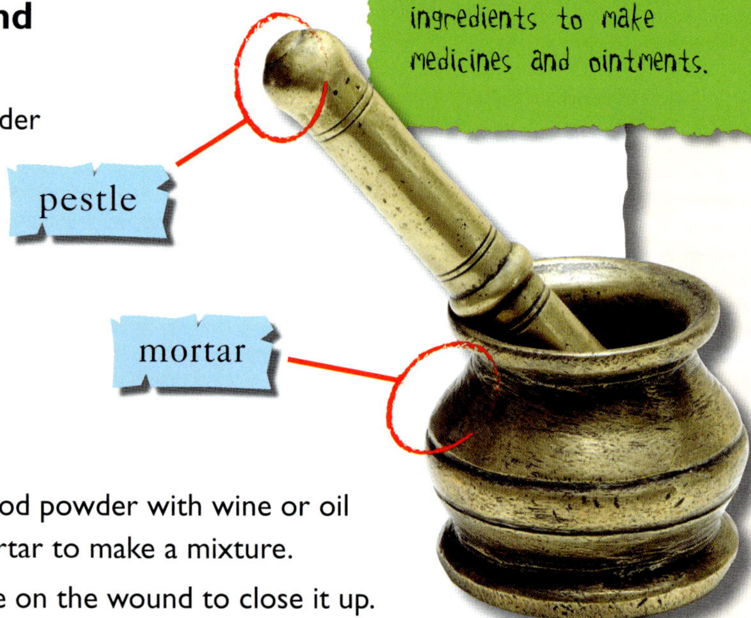

How to do it

1. Grind dragon's blood powder with wine or oil in a pestle and mortar to make a mixture.
2. Spread the mixture on the wound to close it up.

If the wound is large, you must stitch it up. Give the patient a piece of wood to bite on, then sew up the wound.

Removing bullets

You will need:

- forceps
- a thin metal stick
- turpentine or vinegar
- bandage

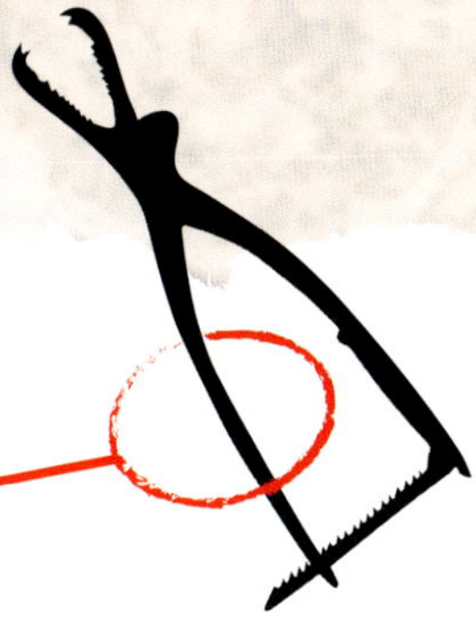

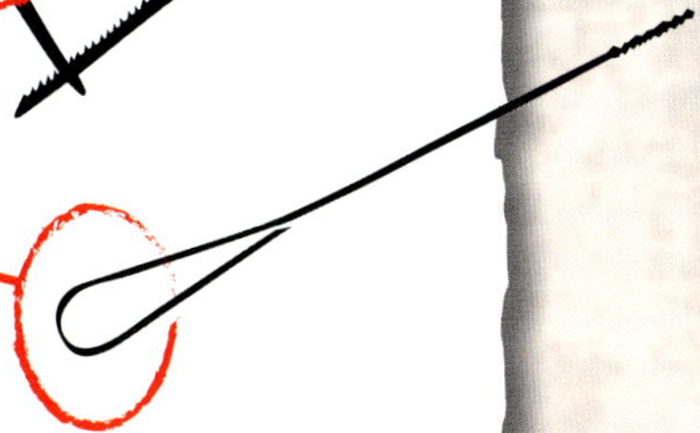

How to do it

1. Using the stick, poke around inside the wound until you find the bullet.
2. Use the forceps to grab the bullet and pull it out.
3. Clean the wound with turpentine or vinegar.
4. Bandage up the area to cover the bullet hole.

dragon tree

"Dragon's blood" doesn't really come from dragons! It is made from the red juice of the dragon tree.

Rotten Wounds

Unfortunately, wounds don't always heal well. If germs get inside, wounds can become **infected**. That means they swell up, hurt, and ooze yucky yellow pus. If **gangrene** sets in, whole body parts start to rot away!

Some bacteria are germs that infect wounds.

Plaster for an infected wound

You will need:

- lard
- olive oil
- dried lavender
- powdered myrrh
- clean cloth

How to do it

1. Mix the ingredients together over a stove.
2. Smear the mixture on to a cloth.
3. Press the plaster against the infected wound, pressing down firmly.

Bloodletting

Another treatment for infected wounds is bloodletting. This means to cause bleeding.

You will need:

- a sharp scalpel or knife
- a blood bowl

Make sure the patient is sitting down. Find a nice big **vein** in the arm and cut into it carefully with your **scalpel**. Catch the blood in the bowl.

Bloodletting used to be a popular medical treatment. Sadly, it didn't really work!

Is it gangrene?

Look out for these signs of grisly gangrene:

- skin turns greenish-black
- flesh starts to cave in and rot
- wound smells really bad!

If a body part has gangrene, turn the page to find out what to do.

Off With His Leg!

Sometimes part of a sailor's body is very badly damaged by gangrene or an injury. Then it has to be **amputated**. That means chopping it right off. That's why you often see old pictures of pirates and sailors with wooden legs or hooks for hands.

axe

Amputating a leg

You will need:

- a tourniquet (strip of cloth)
- a scalpel
- an axe or saw
- a cauterizing iron
- bandages
- opium

If you had a limb amputated in the 1700s, you might still die from an infected stump, bleeding, or shock.

saw

This old painting shows an **officer** about to have an amputation.

How to do it

1. Give your patient plenty of opium or rum.
2. Lay him on a table and have several men hold him still.
3. Tie the **tourniquet** tightly round the leg above the wound, to reduce blood flow.
4. Cut the flesh around the bone with the scalpel.
5. Pull back the flesh so that the bone is sticking out.
6. Saw or chop through the bone.
7. Press a hot cauterizing iron against the leg stump. This stops the bleeding.
8. Wrap the stump tightly in bandages.
9. Give the patient more opium to reduce pain as he recovers.

opium

Hot and Cold

Sailing ships can travel into the most swelteringly hot and icy-cold parts of the world. Getting too hot or cold can be harmful—and even deadly.

Blazing sunshine could roast your crew!

Weather remedies

Have these treatments ready whenever your ship encounters extreme weather.

1. Sunstroke makes sailors dizzy, sick, and faint from the heat.
What to do: Keep the patient in the shade, and use damp cloths to cool him down. Give him cold water to drink.

2. Sunburn makes the skin turn red, blister, and peel.
What to do: Rub aloe vera juice all over the burned area.

aloe vera

3. Exposure means getting much too cold, from winter weather or falling into icy water.
What to do: Put the sailor into a warm room. Remove his wet clothes and lay warm cloths all over him.

4. Frostbite happens when fingers and toes freeze and turn black.
What to do: Amputate the parts.

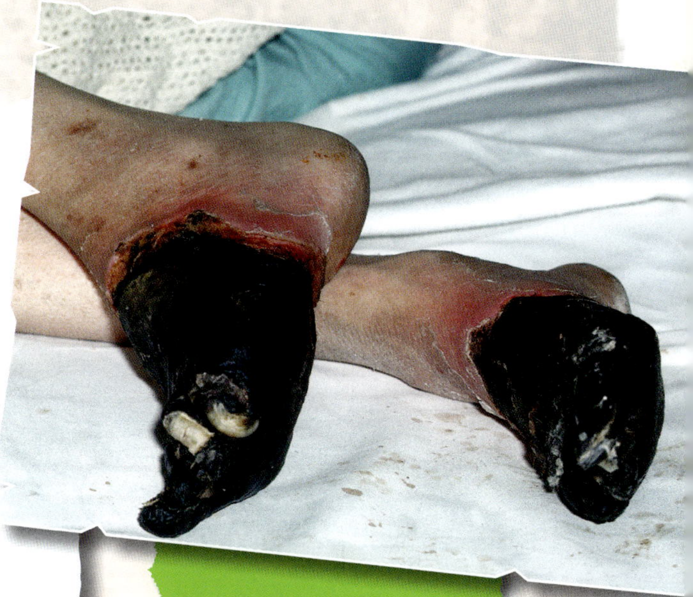

Frostbite can make skin turn black.

Sailor hats!

Many old pictures of sailors and pirates show them wearing wide-brimmed hats or handkerchiefs tied around their heads. These helped to protect them from sunburn and sunstroke.

Scary Scurvy

Many a sailing ship has lost half its men to a terrible illness—scurvy. It is caused by the poor diet that many sailors eat. If it's not treated, it's a killer. Luckily, there's a simple cure.

Spotting scurvy

Look out for these symptoms to see if scurvy is affecting the crew:

- aches and pains
- tiredness and weakness
- dark blotches and bruises
- pale skin
- loose teeth and bleeding gums

Captain James Cook gave his crew pickled cabbage to keep them healthy.

Top Tips

Give your crew pickled cabbage. It is very tasty, and it is great for curing scurvy.

Scurvy treatment

You can cure scurvy by adding any of these foods to the patient's diet:

- lemons, oranges, or limes
- potatoes
- cabbage

To prevent scurvy, the crew should eat fresh fruit and vegetables as much as possible, especially **citrus fruit** and **tamarind**.

Scurvy-busting food was prepared in the ship's kitchen.

James Lind

The captains and surgeons of ships always knew that eating fresh food kept their crews healthier. But it was only in the 1740s that British navy doctor James Lind proved that eating lemons and limes could get rid of scurvy.

All in Your Head

It's well known that sailors cooped up on board ship for months on end can go a little crazy. But don't worry—there are also medicines for this.

Are sailors' tales of sea monsters the result of strange visions?

Calenture

Sailors sometimes get **calenture** when their ships are stuck in one place with no wind. It makes them start seeing things. They may even leap overboard, because they think the sea is a green meadow!

What to do

1. Lock the patient safely in a cabin.
2. Give him a licorice drink made by mixing licorice and hot water.
3. If he doesn't recover, try bloodletting (see page 21).

A cure for sleeplessness and terrors

To cure sleeplessness and fears, there is a very expensive medicine called theriac. It has a lot of ingredients, so most surgeons buy it ready-made from an **apothecary**. However, you could make a simple version using these ingredients:

- a dried snake
- a dried lizard
- cinnamon
- rhubarb
- ginger
- aniseed
- pepper
- cloves
- myrrh
- turpentine
- opium
- wine
- honey

Grind and stir everything together, and give the patient a spoonful a day.

Opium is made from some types of poppy flowers.

Top Tips

Opium is often used as a cure for worries and **depression** because it puts you to sleep.

Glossary

admiral Commander of a fleet of ships

amputate To cut off a body part

apothecary Someone who made and sold medicines

calenture An illness that makes people see things that aren't there

cauterize To seal up a wound with heat

chills Feeling cold and shivery

cholera A serious disease spread by infected drinking water

citrus fruit Oranges, lemons, limes, grapefruits and similar fruit

depression An illness that makes people feel sad and hopeless

dram A small drink

exposure (or hypothermia) The body getting too cold

extract A small, pure amount of something

fever A high body temperature

firearms Guns and cannons

forceps Tool for grabbing and holding

frostbite Damage caused by body parts getting frozen

gangrene Rotting away of living flesh

hallucination Something not real that a person thinks he sees

hostage Someone taken prisoner and released in exchange for something

infected Invaded by disease germs

ipecac A plant that causes vomiting

lance To cut open

malaria Illness causing fever and chills

mercury A silvery metal that is a liquid at room temperature

officer Man in charge on board a ship

ointment Thick, sticky medicine used on the skin

opium Pain-killing substance, made from a type of poppy

pestle and mortar A grinding tool and bowl for crushing ingredients together

plaster A creamy mixture of medicines for smearing on the skin

probe Long needle-like tool

pus Sticky yellow substance that comes out of wounds

remedy A medical cure or treatment

rigging Ropes used to hold up sails

scalpel Small, sharp knife

seasickness Feeling sick because of the movement of a boat

sick bay Area of ship where unwell sailors are treated

sunburn Painful damage to the skin caused by too much exposure to sunlight

sunstroke (or heatstroke) The body overheating

surgeon A doctor who can carry out operations

tamarind Fruit of the tamarind tree, found in Asia

tonic A drug that brings health back

tourniquet A band tied around a body part to slow down bleeding

trepan A drill-like tool for making holes in the skull

vein A type of blood vessel or tube inside the body

Further Information

Web Sites

Read all about the duties of a surgeon aboard a ship in the 1700s at:
www.chesapeakepicaroons.org/DailyLife/medicine.html

Discover the often curious names for diseases in the 1700s at:
http://footguards.tripod.com/01ABOUT/01_sickness.htm#bills

Books

Sail!: Can You Command a Sea Voyage? by Julia Bruce. Enslow Publishers (2009).

A Year on a Pirate Ship by Elizabeth Havercroft. Millbrook Press (2009).

Index